The Cat in the Hat's Learning Library

To Melody with love
—T.R.

The editors would like to thank
BARBARA KIEFER, Ph.D.,
Charlotte S. Huck Professor of Children's Literature,
The Ohio State University, and
DONALD BRUNING, Ph.D., Chairman and Curator,
Department of Ornithology for the Wildlife Conservation Society at the Bronx Zoo,
for their assistance in the preparation of this book.

Visit us on the Web!
www.randomhouse.com/kids
www.seussville.com

Educators and librarians, for a variety of teaching tools, visit us at
www.randomhouse.com/teachers

Library of Congress Cataloging-in-Publication Data
Rabe, Tish.
Fine feathered friends / by Tish Rabe.
    p. cm. — (The Cat in the Hat's learning library)
Summary: Dr. Seuss's Cat in the Hat introduces Sally and Dick to a variety of birds, from the
ten-foot ostrich to the two-inch hummingbird.
ISBN 978-0-679-88362-3 (trade) — ISBN 978-0-679-98362-0 (lib. bdg.)
1. Birds—Juvenile literature. [1. Birds.] I. Title. II. Series.
QL676.2.R316 1998 598—dc21 97-53103

Printed in the United States of America
19

Fine Feathered Friends

by Tish Rabe

illustrated by
Aristides Ruiz

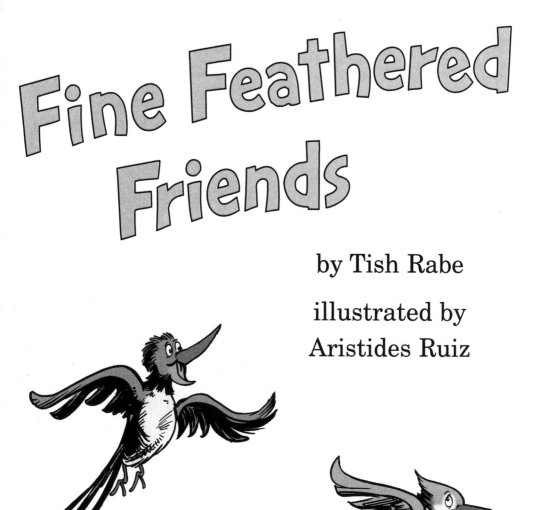

The Cat in the Hat's Learning Library™

Random House New York

I'm the Cat in the Hat,
here to say a few words
about all of your fine feathered friends
known as...

...birds!

There are millions of birds.
I will show some to you.
Your mother
will not mind at all if I do.

Now, the birds we will meet
are alike in some things:
They each have a beak
and a tail
and two wings.

They are covered in feathers
and stand on two legs.
And when they have babies,
they hatch out
of eggs.

Birds have 3 eyelids
on each eye
and have no teeth.
Don't ask us why!

?

Birds come in all colors,
all shapes,
and all sizes,
and live in a world
that is full of surprises!

egg

baby bird

WING

BEAK

FEATHERS

LEGS

TAIL

The world's biggest bird
is the ostrich, you see.
It can stand nine feet tall.
Why, that's taller than me!

There's a tale told about them
I don't understand.
Some say that these birds
hide their heads in the sand.
But they couldn't and wouldn't—
it's simply not true!
It's a thing that no ostrich
I know of would do!

The bee hummingbird
is so tiny, so small.
It's just two inches long.
That's the smallest
of all.

And its wings beat so fast
that they hum when it flies,
and the eggs that it lays
are just…

…jellybean size!

A bird gets its name
from the simplest things:
what it does, how it looks,
or the song that it sings.

Like the flycatcher's name
comes as no big surprise.
Because when it's hungry,
it likes to catch flies!

The chickadee's named
for the sound of its song.
It **chick-a-dee-dees**
in the trees
all day long.

And the beautiful blue jay
you see flying by
has feathers as bright
and as blue as the sky.

15

While the spoonbill,
who lives in a marsh or lagoon,
is named for its bill,
which is shaped like a spoon.

And the tailorbirds far off
in Asia, I've read,
sew up their nests,
but they never use thread.
They shred up thin pieces
of dead leaves instead.

And...

...meet the bald eagle!
I'm happy to say:
He's the national bird
for the whole U.S.A.!
Though his name says he's hairless,
he's really not bald.

He's the symbol of freedom—
whatever he's called.

When you're looking for birds,
you can listen to hear
the sounds that they make
that are new to your ear.

Like the owls who go "hoo"
and the herons who squawk.
Or the doves' gentle coo—
that's the way that they talk.

Or a parakeet's trill
or a guinea hen's cluck,
the boom of an ostrich,
the quack of a duck.
The cry of the loon
or the caw of the crow—
or the catbird
who meows
like some cats that I know.

SQUAWK

HOOooo

Some birds that you see
love to glide through the sky,
while other birds stay on the ground
and can't fly.

Take the New Zealand kiwi
(whose name rhymes with peewee)—
both he-wi and she-wi
will never take flight.

And these shy little birds
like to stay out of sight
and search for their food
in the dark of the night.

Now, birds have some habits
we may think are strange,
but these habits are things
that they can't ever change.

Like the emperor penguins
who live in the snow,
where there's nothing to build
a warm nest with, and so...

...when a mom lays an egg,
it goes up on Dad's feet,
and until it is hatched,
he can't move and can't eat.

He must stand very still
through each cold, icy storm,
till the day finally comes...

...and the baby is born!

Then it's Mom's turn to help,
to take over and keep
an eye on the baby...

...while Dad gets some sleep.

When a male whooping crane
feels it's time for romance,
he hops up and down
in a strange kind of dance.

His wings go **flap flip**
and his feet go **flip flop.**
He twirls and he swirls
with a hip and a hop.

And although you might think
this dance isn't exciting,
a female crane finds it…

…extremely inviting!

When birds want to go
on a winter vacation,
they all take a trip
and they call it migration.

Wild geese are quite good
at this trick, as you see.
They fly off in a flock
in the shape of a "V."

But the bird up in front
gets the wind in his face
and must soon take a rest,
so a friend takes his place.

Then the lead goose falls back,
has a rest, and starts gliding
on air waves his other goose friends
are providing.

Oh, look at the time!

Why, the minutes just flew!

We must get you home.

I know just what to do.

Come on! Follow me!

You will see what I mean.

It's my Fine Feather, All-Weather
Flying Machine!
There is room for you both,
so just hop right on in it.
You'll wing right back home.
You'll be there
in a minute!

Dear Dick and sweet Sally,
oh, how was your day?
Did you have any fun?
Did you learn?
Did you play?

Please tell me about it,
but first...

...a surprise!
I've been to the pet store.
Now quick! Close your eyes!

I bought you a bird!
It's a Ruzzamatuzz.
It's a baby all covered
in soft, downy fuzz.

I don't know much about birds.
Do you know...

...who does?

GLOSSARY

Asia: The largest continent. It is bordered by the Arctic, Pacific, and Indian oceans, and by Europe.

Flock: A group of animals that eat, live, or travel together.

Freedom: The opportunity to think, act, and speak as one pleases.

Lagoon: A shallow body of water usually attached to a larger body of water.

Marsh: Low, wet land where various grasslike plants grow.

Migration: The periodic act of moving from one place to another.

Symbol: Something that stands for something else.

Trill: The rapid singing of a series of similar or alternate sounds.

FOR FURTHER READING

Amazing Birds by Alexandra Parsons, photographed by Jerry Young (Alfred A. Knopf, *Eyewitness Juniors*). Closeup photos of many exotic birds. For grades 1 and up.

The Egg by Gallimard Jeunesse and Pascale de Bourgoing, illustrated by René Mettler (Scholastic, *A First Discovery Book*). All about eggs! For preschoolers and up.

The Little Duck by Judy Dunn, photographed by Phoebe Dunn (Random House, *Picturebacks*). A funny but true story about a year in a duck's life. For preschoolers and up.

A Nest Full of Eggs by Priscilla Belz Jenkins, illustrated by Lizzy Rockwell (HarperTrophy, *Let's-Read-and-Find-Out Science*, Stage 1). American robins make a nest, lay eggs, and care for their chicks. For preschoolers and up.

Owl photographed by Kim Taylor (Dorling Kindersley, *See How They Grow*). Closeup photos follow an owl chick from birth to maturity. For preschoolers and up.

INDEX